What's Different?

Fran Newman-D'Amico

DOVER PUBLICATIONS, INC.
Mineola, New York

Bibliographical Note

What's Different? is a new work, first published by
Dover Publications, Inc., in 2002.

International Standard Book Number

ISBN-13: 978-0-486-42334-0
ISBN-10: 0-486-42334-4

Manufactured in the United States by LSC Communications
42334417   2017
www.doverpublications.com

Note

This little activity book has pictures of busy butterflies, a buzzing bee, a birthday party, and more! To do the puzzles, look carefully at each page on the left. The page facing it on the right looks just the same as the one on the left, but it's not— some things have changed! As you find each thing that's different, draw a circle around it. Try to do all of the pages on your own before you look at the Solutions, which begin on page 58. When you are done, you can enjoy coloring the pages. Remember, look carefully!

Spot is having fun at the park today.

What's different in the picture? Find and circle
5 things that have changed.

Calvin is ready to kick the ball.

What 4 things are different in the picture?
Find and circle them.

These butterflies are enjoying a fine summer day.

Now look at this picture. What has changed?
Circle the 6 things that are different.

Bunny is ready to have a nibble in the
tomato garden.

Some things are different in the picture.
Find the 6 changes and circle them.

11

Here are two playful monkeys.

Now look! Find the 5 things that are different and circle each one.

Charlie is having a great time flying his new kite.

Look again! What has changed in the picture?
Circle the 4 things that are different.

Amanda is making a wish for her birthday.

The picture is different now! Find the 6 things
that have changed and circle them.

Nancy hears the birds singing in her backyard.

The birds still are singing, but 5 things in the picture are different. Can you find and circle them all?

Kevin the Clown enjoys his job with the circus.

Oh no! A lot of things in the picture are
different! Find and circle all 5 changes.

This picture shows Carlos swimming
near the sea creatures.

This picture looks the same, but it isn't. Find the
5 things that are different and circle them.

23

This is a picture of Jamie's four cats.

Now look! There are 6 things different in the
picture. Find and circle them all.

Tina would like to explore space as
an astronaut.

This picture shows Tina, but there are 3 changes.
Find and circle what is different.

It's another fine day at Mrs. Finney's farm.

Look again! Find and circle 5 things that are different in the picture.

Tyrone is having a great time
building a snowman.

Now look at the picture. Find and circle the
5 things that are different.

This backyard certainly is busy today!

Now there are 4 things different. Can you find and circle them all?

Here are Flip and Freddy Frog and
their friend, Emily.

What's different? Find and circle 5 things
that have changed.

Anna is ready to go for a swim.

Look carefully at the picture. Can you find
the 4 things that are different?

Nick and Nelly are posing to have
their picture taken.

Here are Nick and Nelly, but 6 things are
different in the picture. Find and circle them.

Antonio and Maria are giving Peter
his birthday gifts.

This picture looks the same, but it isn't! Find and circle the 4 things that are different.

These barnyard friends like to have a chat
every now and then.

Now the picture looks very different. Find the
4 things that have changed and circle them.

Percy is performing a trick at the circus.

Here is Percy, but 6 things are different in the picture. Circle all 6 things.

Jessie and Jasmine love to skate at the rink.

There are 4 things different in the picture.
Find them all and circle them.

Marcus marches with the band at school.

Marcus still is marching, but 4 things are different in the picture. Circle all the changes.

This tall tree is filled with creatures today!

Take another look. There are 5 things different in the picture. Circle them all.

Princess Patty thinks she hears a parade coming.

Now there are 4 things that have changed in the picture. Find and circle them.

It looks like a good day for taking a swim.

Look carefully at the picture and find the
4 things that are different.

Cool water is just what the Pig family
needs on this hot day!

Now look at the picture. There are 5 differences.
Find and circle them all.

Solutions

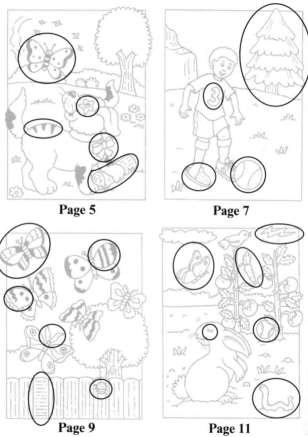

Page 5

Page 7

Page 9

Page 11

Page 13

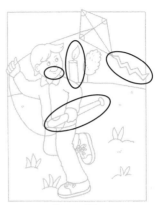

Page 15

Page 17

Page 19

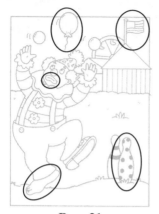

Page 21

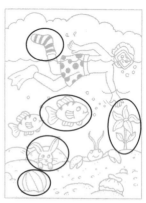

Page 23

Page 25

Page 27

60

Page 29

Page 31

Page 33

Page 35

Page 37

Page 39

Page 41

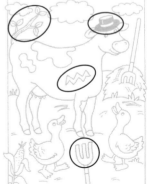

Page 43

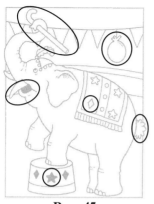

Page 45

Page 47

Page 49

Page 51

Page 53

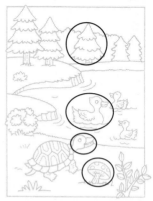

Page 55

Page 57